WINDMILL BOOKS™

I Can Draw
Pets

Contents

Dog

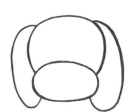

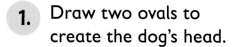

1. Draw two ovals to create the dog's head.

2. Pencil an ear on each side of the head.

3. Add a triangular-shaped body and front paws.

4. On each side of the body, draw a back leg.

5. Draw the dog's curved and pointed tail.

6. Draw details on the paws, chest, ears, and face.

Rabbit

1. Draw a large oval with two ears.

2. Pencil the chest and front legs.

3. Sketch a rounded back and hind leg.

4. Add a cloud-shaped fluffy tail.

5. Draw the face and add details to the ears.

6. Pencil faint lines on the chest and hind leg.

Parrot

1. Draw a curved, tear-shaped wing.

2. Sketch a shape to form the body.

3. Add the front of the second wing.

4. Draw the head and hooked beak.

5. Sketch claws, then the perch and tail feathers.

6. Add details to the face, beak, and feathers.

Chinchilla

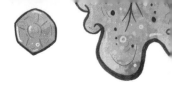

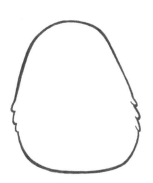

1. Draw the rounded triangular body.

2. Pencil half circles for the ears.

3. Add the feet and sausage-shaped tail.

4. Draw a pair of small, black eyes.

5. Sketch the eyebrows, nose, mouth, and muzzle.

6. Add front paws, whiskers, and shading.

Cat

1. Start by drawing a circle for the head.

2. Add a pair of ears and tabby marks to the head.

3. Pencil the eyes, nose, mouth, and whiskers.

4. Sketch a large oval for the cat's body.

5. Pencil in a rear leg and paw and front paws.

6. Draw a cushion, the tail, more tabby marks, and add shading.

Tortoise

1. Draw a half circle for the shell.

2. Add two short and wrinkly legs.

3. Draw the head and curved neck.

4. At the other end of the shell, draw a stubby tail.

5. Pencil some patterns onto the shell.

6. Finish by adding details to the tortoise's head.

Mouse

1. Draw a petal shape for the head.

2. Add ears and two lines for the body.

3. Draw eyes and brows and detail to the ears.

4. Pencil front paws and a hind leg and paw.

5. Sketch the nose and whiskers.

6. Give your mouse a long, curly tail.

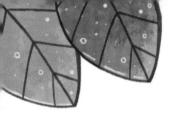

Lizard

1. Draw the lizard's head and snout.

2. Pencil in an eye and brow.

3. Draw body outline and claw-toed feet.

4. Sketch the belly and claw-toed hind legs.

5. Add a long, pointed tail.

6. Add face details and spines to the body and tail.

Guinea Pig

1. Draw a curved shape for the head.

2. Add details to the head and face.

3. Draw the guinea pig's front tooth.

4. Sketch a round, curved tummy.

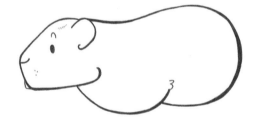

5. Now, draw the rest of the body.

6. Add three tiny feet and details to the ear.

18

Goldfish

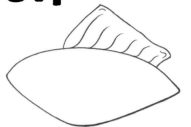

1. Draw a pointed oval for the body.

2. Sketch a spined fin along the top.

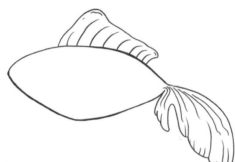

3. Add the tail fin with all its details.

4. Draw two more spined fins on the body.

5. Pencil a gill, brow, eye, and mouth.

6. Lightly sketch scales, shading, and air bubbles.

Parakeet

1. Draw the top of the head and beak.

2. Now draw the eye, nostril, and chin.

3. Add a wing and its layers of feathers.

4. Draw a curved line for the bird's chest.

5. Draw one foot with clawed toes.

6. Draw a second foot, long tail, and perch.

Pony

1. Draw the forehead, muzzle, and jaw.

2. Pencil the eye, brow, and nostril. Add ears with some hair between them.

3. Draw the pony's neck, back, chest, and mane.

4. Draw two hoofed legs and a curved tummy.

5. Add two more hoofed legs.

6. Sketch the long, flowing tail.

Hamster

1. Draw the nose, eyes, brows, and paws.

2. Add the ears and a slice of carrot.

3. Draw the top of the head and extend the paws.

4. Draw the hamster's rounded, furry body.

5. Sketch a pair of large hind paws.

6. Add fat cheeks, whiskers, and detail to the body.

Snake

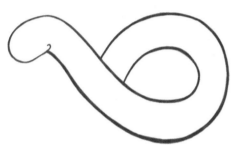

1. Draw a long, curling body with a head.

2. Pencil eyes and nostrils on the head.

3. Now draw the snake's tail.

4. Draw stripes across the body and tail.

5. Shade in every second stripe.

6. To finish, give your snake a forked tongue.

Llama

1. Draw a neck, head, muzzle, and ear.

2. Add a mouth, eye, and second ear to the head.

3. Draw the llama's furry back and chest.

4. Pencil a hoofed leg, tummy, and tail.

5. Add a second hoofed front leg.

6. Draw two hind legs. Add shading to the fur.

Published in 2019 by Windmill Books,
an Imprint of Rosen Publishing
29 East 21st Street, New York, NY 10010

Created and Produced by Green Android Limited
Illustrations by Grace Sandford

Cataloging-in-Publication Data

Names: Sandford, Grace.
Title: I can draw pets / Grace Sandford.
Description: New York : Windmill Books, 2019. | Series: I can draw
Identifiers: ISBN 9781538390184 (pbk.) | ISBN 9781508197300 (library bound) | ISBN
9781538390191 (6 pack)
Subjects: LCSH: Animals in art--Juvenile literature. | Drawing--Technique--Juvenile
literature.
Classification: LCC NC783.8.P48 S264 2019 | DDC 743.6--dc23
Manufactured in the United States of America

CPSIA Compliance Information: Batch BW19WM: For Further Information contact Rosen Publishing,
New York, New York at 1-800-237-9932